In the final year of my 40s

Also by Simon Perril

Poetry

Hearing is Itself Suddenly a Kind of Singing
A Clutch of Odes
Nitrate
Newton's Splinter
Archilochus on the Moon *
Beneath *

Criticism

The Salt Companion to John James
Tending the Vortex: The Works of Brian Catling

An asterisk denotes a Shearsman title.

In the final year of my 40s

Simon Perril

Shearsman Books

First published in the United Kingdom in 2018 by
Shearsman Books
50 Westons Hill Drive
Emersons Green
BRISTOL
BS16 7DF

Shearsman Books Ltd Registered Office
30–31 St. James Place, Mangotsfield, Bristol BS16 9JB
(this address not for correspondence)

www.shearsman.com

ISBN 978-1-84861-614-1

Cover image by the author, plate from *Under Austerity Rubble,
Ancestral Bird-folk Lay Future Eggs.*

In the final year of my 40s

In the final year of my 40s
I shall abdicate responsibility
for all my poems say, do, or be
so they might get a life
away from me.

In the final year of my 40s
I shall dial up the sea, knowing
it doesn't like to talk
and I will court ridicule
from lesser folk.

In the final year of my 40s
all these creatures I love : teals
and tapirs, claude toads, capybara,
binturong, will still have no place in my poems
and I won't know why.

In the final year of my 40s
my poems, oh my poems!
Where will you be hiding, how
will you tease me so
always pointing beyond my reach.

In the final year of my 40s
I shall have no truck with tables, charts
strike no truce with numbers
yet forge a tryst
with the sexual favours of sunlight.

In the final year of my 40s
I shall mislay myself,
fumble for an alternative, miss
that other and rediscover
the stranger inside and own him.

In the final year of my 40s
I shall accommodate my disappointments
in an outhouse. There
they will be free to live
a full, frank and unfettered life.

In the final year of my 40s
I may, just may, transcribe
the folksongs of kitchen implements,
gravel and pockets – just as it's
rarely done well.

In the final year of my 40s
I shall inquire. Not of the opening
of evenings past spring. Nor
the drawing of shadows before
and behind standing things. I shall
just inquire, head slightly decanted.

In the final year of my 40s
I shall spend longer in bed seeking the channel
between curtain and wall, left of my head,
that squeezes the prospect
of tree and hill adjacent to Brooke Hill.

In the final year of my 40s
I shall spend less time
fretting in my poems
like an awkward barre chord
my straining finger cannot hold.

In the final year of my 40s
I shall write to today
perpetually, and by appointment
and shun the lack of attention
due to me.

In the final year of my 40s
I shall install a parliament of sighs
with the express purpose of documenting
and hearing the expressed purposelessness
of the wage-slaved.

In the final year of my 40s
I shall successfully burn said parliament
liberate the sighs,
and apologise to those left outside
the relative warmth of work.

In the final year of my 40s
I'll take off. Really, momentarily
I'll leave the ground. You've not seen my wings,
my shoulders itch with them. They're
nondescript in colour. Who am I to boast.

In the final year of my 40s
I shall toast the next 40 as it's good
to do things early, it leaves
unforeseen spaces for poems to populate.
Besides, being late makes me nervous.

In the final year of my 40s
I shall discover a new colour
and keep it to myself. Perhaps
I'll bury it in the garden
and the grass will breathe its rumour.

In the final year of my 40s
'pioneering', 'award winning'
'capable of moving even
inanimate objects closest to your loved ones'
– none of the above accolades will serve my books.

In the final year of my 40s
I shall not reconcile my quandary
over names; and whether there is shame
in not having them to hand when you call
for the small things to which you are kin.

In the final year of my 40s
under controlled conditions I shall
turn myself inside out and back again. Few
will know, though under certain lights
my lines will show the burden of such transformation.

In the final year of my 40s
I shall often think
of Abel Gance's La Bussière
Eater of Documents; he
who digested paper terrors.

In the final year of my 40s
I shall recycle sleep.
I shall knit my wife
a four poster bed
from the fleece of miscounted sheep.

In the final year of my 40s
I shall frequently ponder Auerbach's
articulation of the 'last bout';
the stamina, the training required
to remain in vexed, effervescing light.

In the final year of my 40s
I shall feel more charitable
towards things posing as themselves.
Let them be. Turn away,
and listen to what they say.

In the final year of my 40s
I shall join the British Association
of Equine Dental Technicians
so as to file, rasp, and de-clutter
the horse's mouth; restore its bite ratio.

In the final year of my 40s
I shall discover Francis Bacon's lost locked
sea chest, and do my best to pry it open:
pliers, intense fires, controlled explosions,
colourful language, will all prove useless.

In the final year of my 40s
I shall greet Mr Jones, and congratulate him
on his continued promotion since '65
knowing something is happening
and the full horror of knowing what it is.

In the final year of my 40s
I shall attend to the envelope.
I shall push and prod at the envelope;
I shall burn the envelope, hide the envelope,
then deny the envelope ever existed.

In the final year of my 40s
my thoughts shall frequently lie down,
shed their weight, adopt the elegant gait
of a deerhound suspended
above the ground under its feet.

In the final year of my 40s
I shall marry the woman I tried to walk to
30 years back, trudging my teen-self
'cross the toe-path of the Stort
till it dusked, and I could no longer trust my outline.

In the final year of my 40s
Elly will walk down a castle aisle to me
in the smallest county in England
and we'll crowd-fund elation
to the croons of Dr John.

In the final year of my 40s
I shall float free from my verses, stretch
the distance between voice and amplification
like clouds below a plane
shun their shadow.

In the final year of my 40s
Elly and I shall honeymoon on a Marrakech rooftop
under grammatically correct skies
and a small bird will whisper
the secret of the mixture for Marjorelle Blue.

In the final year of my 40s
I shall challenge Euclid to account for the geometry
of North African rooftops; quiz Schrödinger
on the quantum transit of his cats through the alleys
of Marrakech, blinking particles and waves.

In the final year of my 40s
I shall swim in a roof top pool
shared with my wife and the passing lips of swallows
in the shadow of La Katoubia; and the water
will hold a different blue from the sky.

In the final year of my 40s
I shall write only in ink
siphoned from the implied black
in the bluebell. See
this sample here:

In the final year of my 40s
I shall propose exasperation as the new renewable
harvested by wind farms
and gusts of shuffled forms
generated in institutional rooms.

In the final year of my 40s
I shall flavour my poems
grant them transformative tangs
exquisite textures
that modify the mouth.

In the final year of my 40s
these flavours shall be: liquorice root,
kiwi fruit, menthol, chilli,
tastes that play in the cave
of a mouth slightly ajar.

In the final year of my 40s
let there be commerce between each and all.
My poems shall CC everybody,
everything; and usher in
a remembrance of things to come.

In the final year of my 40s
these ceilings shall not prevent
star-scent travelling
the length of my tunnelled nostrils
nor the resulting sneeze.

In the final year of my 40s
these folk whose business extends
to the co-mingling in a single box
of separate, incompatible jigsaw skies
shall be less despised.

In the final year of my 40s
bless all the edges
without whom nothing
can connect with nothing. Hail
all forms of joining.

In the final year of my 40s
my poems shall cultivate
buoyancy; draw pacts with water,
aim for the meander of dust motes
adrift in light's butter.

In the final year of my 40s
I shall sit for the ticking day, talking
whilst it insists I still
this volatility of face
racing out its shapes.

In the final year of my 40s
I shall refuse to sit for the poem
knowing its constitution
to be wrong for the weather front
of words coming in.

In the final year of my 40s
bring me feathers and a song
to catch in my craw
that opens like a door
onto a rhythm of fields.

In the final year of my 40s
I shall build on those fields
humble dwellings; they'll
snore a descant
for our daily chores.

In the final year of my 40s
I shall wake shrink-wrapped
dreaming of Cecil Taylor
playing Scriabin's 10th Sonata
for insects, pages turned by Gregor Samsa.

In the final year of my 40s
I shall intercede in the early-houred
bickering of cats, with such fluency
the neighbourhood will bestow upon me
the role of Chief Negotiator.

In the final year of my 40s
the establishment of my School
For The Caterwaul will have few takers
and the whiskered fraternity henceforth
shall regard me as an opportunistic traitor.

In the final year of my 40s
I shall sleep on my side
– an ergonomically driven decision,
advancing upon the duck's back
the dream-ducts that furrow the page.

In the final year of my 40s
the sculptural challenge shall be
branching into self-portraiture,
shaping who I intend to be
through the medium of cold tea bags.

In the final year of my 40s
that receptacle I keep
for all life throws at me
I shall dump in the garden, hoping
to not ape Blake's poison tree.

In the final year of my 40s
I'll likely wake to no additional distraction
transforming the garden
yet the enforced clear-out
will have done me good.

In the final year of my 40s
my failure to write a new poetics
founded upon ergonomics
will permit my poems
a greater grace and idiocy.

In the final year of my 40s
ban the self-evident,
bolster the resolve
of glassed water lipped: I shall
have none of it explained.

In the final year of my 40s
this mystery of holding;
wavering grasp, un-imperious grip
that fails, falls, flails:
I shall model it.

In the final year of my 40s
I shall wake from uneasy dreams
and find myself a neatly boxed,
immaculately columned form
– cerise vital stats clutched, intact.

In the final year of my 40s
that tract I hammer away at
on the dermatological consequences
of interactions with the page
shall cause an outrage I shall store.

In the final year of my 40s
I shall call upon this affront
as an essential ingredient
inject it straight
into my lyric gland.

In the final year of my 40s
more of the looking out
and the letting in. More
of the facing front
and a feeling for edges.

In the final year of my 40s
I shall camp at the borders
of the poem, issue papers
to guerrilla forces intent
on overthrowing the word.

In the final year of my 40s
I shall smuggle poems
into the smallest spaces,
cracks, cornices and crevices; poems
tattooed to the genitals of mice.

In the final year of my 40s
my wife and I shall discuss
the composition of my headstone, led
by the lines she best recalls from my work.
She will quip: 'I remember the Hermes bits.'

In the final year of my 40s
my wife and I, sousvid in the small hours,
shall read Tomaž Šalamun by pink torchlight
and wake recalling rabbits
wearing antlers, and hens on their side.

In the final year of my 40s
I shall take out dual citizenship and reside
in the lower annex of my secondary imagination
on a dusty chair Coleridge couldn't possibly
regard as esemplastic.

In the final year of my 40s
I shall write poems that swab
the tip of the tongue, teasing
for the tug of the word to come.
Test results shall prove null.

In the final year of my 40s
I shall pioneer the stanza as frame;
nothing to do with film, just the square
of a window onto nothing
but that space top left, just there:

In the final year of my 40s
neglect the book you dip into
reject the book you lose yourself in
for the new class of poem
you fall from.

In the final year of my 40s
my hunt for the hat that
pitying critics passed to Poe
on refusing to publish 'The Raven'
shall grow in both intensity and futility.

In the final year of my 40s
my poems shall desert, abscond
on their overtones; career
through the undergrowth faking
their papers desperately carrying donor cards.

In the final year of my 40s
I'll show no surprise
as my poems file for bankruptcy
and strip themselves of sonic assets.
I'll show neither surprise, nor mercy.

In the final year of my 40s
the elaborate lengths I'll go to
writing when the hours are at their smallest
will veer just this side of mania, mining
the paraphernalia locked in the shells of shape.

In the final year of my 40s
I shall wake many times
and each of them will bear
their own unique insignia
stamped somewhere you'll never find.

In the final year of my 40s
however much I gaze at the early watercolours
of Joseph Beuys, the mystery
of their liquid suspension shall elude me. Yet,
they will continue to hold me whilst they dance.

In the final year of my 40s
a brief spell in court
shall find me accused
of secreting a stash of stolen glances
sewn into the lining of poems.

In the final year of my 40s
I shall not quite abandon thought
but simplify it just so
the effort-to-reward-ratio
will tip in my favour.

In the final year of my 40s
I shall never achieve lines
with the finely falling quality
rain obtains in the engravings
of Édouard Riou.

In the final year of my 40s
'prehistoric reliefs' shall not form
the title of my New and Selected Poems
and yet I'll savour the flavour
this idea will grant future work.

In the final year of my 40s
I shall steal impetus
at any given moment:
all poetry is theft left
for future generations to prosecute.

In the final year of my 40s
I shall wake in the festive season
at 5, and drink Thames-tinted tea
and journey through İlhan Berk
fingers sticky with mincemeat and pastry.

In the final year of my 40s
I shall train expensive cameras
on the four corners of the page, and sleep.
Time-lapse photography will study
the white world and its activity for me.

In the final year of my 40s
these tapes will be stolen and emerge
as an influence on the development
of artificial intelligence. Science shall study
the self-conscious page.

In the final year of my 40s
my retort shall be to strap
an unintrusive cam to the back
legs of sound particles, just to see
where the words run unattended.

In the final year of my 40s
I shall stop writing this.
Yet the emphasis on serving occasion
to itself, shall form an unobtrusive shelf
for my words to recline upon.